To the memory of Geoff Stevens

I would like to thank the editors of the following magazines in which some of these poems have been published: Acumen, Borderlines, The Dawntreader, Equinox, The Interpreter's House, Iota, the North, Pennine Platform, Poetry Monthly, Purple Patch, Orbis and South.

I would also like to thank the help, support and suggestions of Maggie Holliday.

Previous publication:

away (*Poetry Monthly Press, 2010*)

CONTENTS

The Amen of Knowledge

Going

And she's gone.
I can't tell you where
or when she'll be back.
But here's a few clues.
Here's her ski boots,
there's her woollen sweater,
here's the scarf I bought in Prague
and there's the ballgown
I've to take to the cleaners,
precise instructions attached.
Well you don't need a ballgown
when you're off to fight in the wars.

Not that she's fighting.
She's there for the wounded,
she'll strip the bloody clothing
from any bloody skin
and stripping an assault rifle
was taught as a precaution.
A precaution against what?
I know against what.
All those jerks finding themselves,
shooting into manhood,
those guys know what they want
and it's not TLC from a blonde.

I wandered into the kitchen
getting a feel for emptiness,
putting her mug away,
it's only a few months.
Finding themselves for god's sake,
and then finding her,
ten quid in a tin hat lottery,
she just won't get it.

And then I found the envelope,
under the phone,
the last Will and Testament,
left when I left her alone.

Getting the Point

It's getting to the point
of a small rearrangement
in how things were.
Not exactly a lie,
I did have a girlfriend,
she was called Eileen,
and she did, does, live in Hammersmith.
But she didn't,
as far as I know,
drive a Ferrari
into the lake at Kew Gardens
after an argument
about a duel I'd fought
with Simon Armitage
about her honour
or the placing of a comma
in the Dead Sea poems.
One or the other
it doesn't matter.
The point is that these days
you need an edge,
a little something
that's hard to find
in another poem
about finding your Father's pipe
or a lost letter from a lost love
about snow falling in Blackburn
or a night spent talking
about that Al Gore film.

Cambois, Northumberland

North of Blyth
is another name
just as delicate
redolent of French lace
a light breeze
couples reading Proust
on a terrace
overlooking woodland

and there is
a certain delicacy
in lines on the map
the black capillaries
of railway sidings
where coal mingled
with the village
and the Miners' Institute

that's still there
a fine building
fronting a landscape
flayed to a point
where veins remain
kept alive by walkers
and dogs scampering
on a decent beach

which is all
a little bit obvious
a word scribbled
in a notebook
and even that's spoiled
when the bus driver said

they call it Cammuss
they might do
but here's a cutting
from the evening paper

residents reject
a clean coal plant
and certain jobs
calling for a green future
for them and their children

that's Cammuss
but it isn't
not really
not on the map
or looking back
by someone passing through
that's a village
a community
that only others call Cambois.

Harris Museum and Art Gallery, Preston

You always pause at the Curiosity Shop,
Elwell RA (1929)
face close to the frame,
part of the picture,
bringing a tea for Gran,
telling her again
that I'd get rid of the nosy gits.
But I'm not there,
I'm standing in Grimshaw's shoes,
ankle deep in leaves,
nodding to the woman and child
while my eyes half closed in the gold light
always return to the door,
the door in the high wall,
hiding that house and garden,
his secret while my secret
is breathing out slowly,
too softly to disturb the leaves,
till I feel a part of it all,
not the Harris, 1892,
but the other Harris,
the one with connections,
that's part of the Louvre
and it's part of us,
we're part of the Tate
and it's part of us,
part of the Met
and it's part of us,
the pendulum has its small effect,
Foucault would be pleased,
though where it fits
is open to debate,
as long as it's a quiet one.

Accountants

2 sheep plus
3 goats plus
1 bushel of wheat
equals what?

I don't know,
I don't even know what a bushel is
and neither did these guys in Uruk
who had a bit of a problem
explaining that one of their goats
had already been sold
to a bloke from Lagash
and they only had enough tokens left
for three jars of oil
and this stupid sod from Kish
still didn't get it
till they pressed them down
on a bit of clay
which seemed to help
so they did it again
just to show off
to their mates in the pub
and would you believe it
it caught on
and the next thing is
they're selling the farm
doing whole tablets of the stuff
so their neighbours
could count whatever
while they charged a fortune
then putting in security
after the not so stupid
son of the sod from Kish
scraped a sheep shape

off the waxy surface
which they couldn't prove
so they baked them
which stopped that nonsense
and then they got a bit cocky
adding symbols they made up
for this girl in Umma
they both fancied
till her dad replied
using even clearer signs
that he's also made up
so they made some more
and before you know it
there's scrabble and lawyers
and Carol Ann Duffy.

Gone

But when she's back
there'll be changes.
The fridge won't have stains
loosely based
on the constellation Pleiades.
Library books will not be liable
to fines of 42p.
I've learnt what to do
when we go shopping
and she's suddenly not there.

I can airmail
she'll write back
sale at M&S
must have that coat.
Just seen Nicola.
The poem about Aberystwyth
needs a comma
at the end of line three.
War is great.
We're talking again.

She can't tell me about work,
what platoon was bombed,
who lost a leg,
so we correspond.
Pages about books, car maintenance,
the neighbour's trip to Dublin.
And there's lots to talk about
if I can't understand
a simple request
for two garden gnomes in a war zone.

Allergy (Written in a Country Churchyard)

The pollen tells the tale of parting day
The flowing nose winds slowly to a sneeze
The tissue upwards prods its weary way
And leaves are worlds of darkness in a wheeze.

Tempest in Avenham Park
(for Dean Taylor Theatre)

rough magic
is still magic
if it spells a day
that is far from still

a morning
when storms have spirited
the prints of evening green
bringing me here
to wander this island
where the sharp crack
of a falling leaf
has me turning
searching for bare feet
as they flit their scene again

but it's not to be
and all that's left
has been left at home
the same words
on a printed page
magic enough
but not enough
for this mind to conjure
what isn't here or there

where a play's the place
bounded by my own boundaries
needing the release
of voices pressed to paper
bringing the players
to bring this island
back to my stage again.

Stonehenge

On a sunny day
this place is great,
you can walk for miles,
the kids are safe,
sometimes they come back
loaded down with berries
or eggs from the next valley.
But when it rains
or the cold weather starts
we don't need the journeys,
so, yes, it's a good idea,
all the things we want
under one single roof,
there's lots of choice,
a place for the cart.
I'm not sure about
the endless harp music
but nothing's perfect.

'Willesden Sunset'

Danby's painting
is not for sale

you can't buy
his winter trees
the buildings
that curious look
on a man's face

leave it
there's no price
not on this one

it's not the music
of a Willesden Suite
or a novel
based on the Jubilee Line

it won't be played
at the Wigmore Hall
or found on the shelves
of Cricklewood Library

this one is not for sale
it's for later
when a touch will tell
that these strokes
belonged to him

when all that's left
are blank walls
a bank balance
empty bottles
and a promise to keep in touch.

Back

To two bottles
of semi skimmed a day,
there's another station
on the bathroom radio,
tissues are disappearing
and for some reason
the curtains have been cleaned.
She's back home,
her summer of war
a faded uniform
and stories camouflaged
by the Official Secrets Act.

I know she wasn't fighting,
how many times was I told,
but in between the days
of film shows and 10K runs
was the hard stuff,
the bit about men dying,
the effects of a fixed bayonet,
about nursing in a battlefield,
the bit she won't tell me,
so this isn't right,
I'm looking for signs of stress
and there's nothing to see.

Except the photos,
the few photos I've seen
and I wasn't looking for stress
I was looking for excuses,
the same face in focus,
a man's back turning to a door,
too close and whose door.
I'm not going to ask,

she's here and she's home
but I'm still looking for signs
and every day I'm certain
that she'll find a few of mine.

It Could Have Been Moonlight

Walking the river path
after the movie
was right
letting images fade
in their own time
until you pointed
and for a second
we were stones again
washed by a perfect
ripple of seats

you whispered
it could have been moonlight

as across the water
a neon played
with a high tide
we smiled
full of illusions
that night.

Learning French

When I was a boy
wanting to dive off
the top board at Stechford Baths
I used to climb up
and ask passing strangers
to gently push me off.
That's what it feels like
here on the stairs
terrified to move
so before you go
let me try again
I think I'm ready
but I'll need a touch
a few words in a new language
and if the words aren't there
I can ask,
I can do that.
But I'll need that touch,
I know what I'm like,
without that push
my fear will leave me rigid
hanging on to a coffee cup
as you close the door
silent in the empty spaces
telling myself that this time
I'll have to go back
that this time
the passing stranger has passed.
Que cette fois
l' étranger de passage a passé.

The Birthday Present

is now the past
part of a photo
on the first page
of an album
that's on the photo
one of the presents
that's part of a past
next to a shirt
that I've never worn
which makes you smile

till you had to ask
did I still have yours
and you had to see
that look of despair
as I stare at the print
something about a box
there's an empty yellow box
something from you
something
but my past is not catching up
I have to ask
and you turn the page
which worries me more
than the loss
of a failing memory

Washing Up

The yellow marigold gloves
are slightly too small
one of the compromises
that make up a marriage
like meeting his mates
or taking a call
when you're washing up
and he's reading the Sunday papers

or asking who it was
when you're not interested
watching the dog chase squirrels
through the kitchen window
hearing a chair scrape
as he clears a space
and says it was the girl
he's been seeing for the last two years

not breaking the rhythm,
plate, cup and saucer
while he tells you of the guilt,
white plates, yellow gloves,
how he needs your forgiveness,
the rhythm of the gloves,
I'll be keeping the dog then
breaking more than silence.

On Line Dating

The difficult bit
is the smile,
so thank god for digital cameras.
Two hours and four mirrors
for a self timed natural look
of caring warm sincerity.

After that
the words are a breeze
and so they should be
imagery and rhythm
that space between the lines
the bit that's waiting
to be what you want it to be
which by now is obviously me.

And I'm looking for a woman
who isn't fun loving
young for her age
who doesn't like
walking in the rain
on a beach
under a full moon
while boring me senseless
with a wicked sense of humour
before driving herself
back to Camden
to dry those stupid shoes
before a late booking
at that so new Cambodian bistro.

And if you think
I've got the nerve
to actually put that down

then please email
all letters answered
photo essential
or if guaranteed even slight likeness
to Meg Ryan (circa Sleepless in Seattle)
please ignore above
and contact direct
on 822649.

Costume Design Exhibition
(Yorkshire Coast College)

where did that go
three years
blurred
in the staccato
of needle points
and the hand stitched seconds
of long hems of evening

when all the work's
right here
set
in centre stage
in the soliloquy
of a ball gown
or the side splitting
fun of a corset

where light and sound
add a final touch
to years you'll never forget
though it won't be tonight
you'll take with you
it will be ties
friends that are close
holding together
much more than stays.

Three Women

I'm in Dorset
on a train in Bradford
turning a page
as they reach my table
and fill up the seats

I turn to the window
and hope they're commuters
or out for a day in Leeds
resigning myself to Yorkshire
and the latest on grandchildren

or even worse
as without a word
three hands reach
into three bags
for three mobile phones

and come out
with three novels
that are silently opened
silently read
and Lyme Regis is the next stop.

Proof

I once met a man
who could prove he was sane
he needed that proof
before flying his plane
I naturally asked
what it was that he flew
he casually said
it's a B52.
To hide my surprise
I replied it's my round
cursing my girlfriend
and the old friend she'd found
but what made it worse
was it wasn't the last
she needed to stay
to catch up with her past
so that left no choice
which was sort of okay
as part of me prayed
that he'd do or he'd say
something that proved that
this proof that he needed
was nothing but proof
of how they'd succeeded
in proving a man
can be brainwashed to think
that bombing's a job
to forget in a drink.
But that feeling passed
as the evening went by
and soon it was clear
why she still liked the guy
with his battered tweeds
and his easy laughter

he made me forget
the proof I was after.
Which didn't last long
as in dawn's early light
he was back to work
and all thoughts of last night
were lost in a blast
that passed over our room
and my girlfriend joked
it was safe to assume
he was on his way
to his home on the range
and what did I think
did I think it was strange
we could like a man
and yet hate what he did
which left me no choice
or none that seemed valid
so I said that's true
that I did like the man
but for me that's it
for whatever began
whatever he'd prove
I would never forget
the sound we'd just heard
and whenever we met
I'd see through the charm
and I'd have to accept
some share of the cost
with each drink that he bought
and then feel the shame
when I'd read the report
of a wedding bombed
in a surgical strike
and know that no words
could now prove what's that like

to someone whose passed
by a proof he won't see
so meet all you want
but it won't be with me.

Part

At the last rehearsal
the actress looks the part
carefully dressed in innocence
flowers on blue cotton
there's nothing much to do
move that table
take a break
the sleeves of my dress
could be two inches longer

could be must be
there's nothing much to say
and no one will hear
as you turn on the lights
in your spare room
at the back of midnight

two inches is four inches
of stitching and coffee
an hour an inch
but don't think about that
because she won't
and what does it matter
the play's the thing
this is your part

and you know it well
know as the curtains rise
the audience won't read
your unwritten lines
and at two a.m.
you take a break
wrap your fingers
round a warm mug.

Paediatric Life Support Exam

multiple choice
but you've already chosen

head down
blanking the banter
of uniform humour

this is a tough one
not your field

as hard as understanding
why you have to go
again

no simple answers
not even as easy
as not dyeing
the grey in your hair

that wasn't meant
the bit about dyeing
it's too close
and it's not about you
not entirely
but I think I'll keep it there

and I'll wave you off
when you pass
as you will
we all know
children can't be failed

hand your papers in

Maggie Sees a Seagull in Sainsburys (Scarborough)
(or 2 for the price of 1)

1.

From what she said
no one asked
whether it was for sale
buy one get one
free as a bird
fresh today
a Kittiwake
only from Sainsburys
Common Terns
are available from Lidls
in Bridlington or Filey

2.

Why didn't the little so and so
just shove off through the exit door
it's not difficult
even the bosses managed that
before it was their problem
and damn well quicker than the bloody thing
could shift from Household Goods
to the top of the Freezers
and that's going to be a pain
if it's messed up there
what was it thinking of
does it say Linda McArtney Pier
enjoy the view
wave after wave of shelves
breaking round those claws
well they're breaking here as well mate
breaking the not so bleeding heart
of the one with the mop
the one whose thinking
of what rhymes with bucket.

Dave's Point

Last week
was the Battle of Britain
dogfights between jobs
someone said Polish squadrons
had the highest kill rate

Tuesday's tea break
was a brief skirmish
between India and Pakistan
but it was hard work
no one really cares about cricket
not when City are struggling

today
the new bloke
asked about the cuts
and everything stopped
as Dave went on one,
job losses, fat cats, tax cheats,
breaking Britain, blood on the streets,
this wasn't Dave

Dave does cycling,
chats up Reps,
Dave doesn't fill a silence
with thoughts of a poem,
a decent poem,
about Robins,
winner of some national prize

that just then
seemed quite ridiculous
as much use as poesy,
stuff we'd clear

from the filters of blocked pumps,
which is my point,
but not much of a one,
not compared to Dave's.

Joe's Café

is on a secret beach
don't tell,
the sort of beach
the Famous Five found
while searching for clues
on a hot day in June
when they desperately needed
shade and lashings of ginger beer
all thoughts of adventure
cool on the terrace of Joe's Café.

But don't tell,
Mum's the word
and Dad's the word
and children are shrieks of water
splashing on treasure in boxes
left by pirates
or the girls at Joe's Café.

Don't tell friends
or your neighbours flying to Greece
that some things change
and some things don't,
that the hard white paths
high on Ballard Down
will still be contrails
when all that's left
won't matter
not when there's organic
or non-organic
ginger beer and croissants
and hanging out at Joe's Café.

Narrow Lane in Guernsey

Diving into hawthorn
instead of Moulin Huet

counting the pricks
in a passing place

tuning the radio
to dull the pain

a panel's discussing
Thomas Robert Malthus

they don't know an island
with forty thousand cars.

Pre-Deployment Service
208 Field Hospital (Volunteers)

So
what did
the Romans do for us?
     (Sermon: the Padre)

Well
not York Minster
for a start
but any decent fisher
of men or women
baits a hook

and waits
for the line to twitch
the ranks
family and friends
even doubters
ready to be reeled in
by parables of peace and justice

and in the nave later
passing strangers
are more than happy
to press this button here
for small groups
ranked round loved ones
caught between two lives
till a final amen has them leaving
turning to wave
as they turn into Minster Yard
transformed in that short distance
from what we know
to another form of service.

Sand

Pure sand is silica
formed from rock
weathered down
ground down
to less than a millimetre
the size of a full stop.

But punctuation
doesn't write a novel
deserts are sand
stories traced
in infinite lines.

Sand is the poetry
of isolated coves
or the beach at Bournemouth
on a May Day Holiday.

Sand is silica
and not always pure
its smooth bare dunes
punctuated by drills dipped
into blue black ink
selling itself
signing contracts
that promise constancy
swearing a life together
divorced from reality.

Conference of the Association for the Study of Peak Oil
(Cork, Ireland)

What do you do
after a tough day
of World Oil Resources,
of Global Energy Demand Trends
and you're miles away
mind and body relaxing
when up to the next urinal
steps the ex
Head of the CIA?

Well, you don't think
of Fossil Fuels or Carbon Capture,
the consequences of the end of cheap energy
dramatically fade away
as you wait
for the door of the gents to shatter
and men in balaclavas to pour in
screaming at me to assume the position.

I've got a position
I've got a position
Tradeable Quotas
an Energy Descent Plan
Termination with Extreme Prejudice
Time to Shut Up
but it was okay
he just nodded, washed his hands
and left with all the questions
I've thought of since
like why wasn't I ready
when the point of the conference was
it's time to react.

Wishful Thinking

Have you still
got the dress
I almost
bought you

or did you
throw it out
with all
the other stuff

Before the Game

Leaning against the wall
waiting for my mates
the rough red brick
of the toolmaker's yard
stains my jacket
like it did the last time
and the time before
and the time in the twenties
when other shoulders
turned to light Woodbines
in the lee of the crowd
the smoke soon lost
in the up line steam
that shadows the bodies
crossing the bridge
into the first noise
of the main stand
behind me
where two kids
swap cards
dodging a horse
as the copper leans
to cheek a woman
with three scarves
the boys of '64
share chips
buying a programme
from the same spot
as they did last time
and the time before
the dust from my jacket
brushed off
for another layer
to our history.

The Smell of Toast

Urgent

which was fine by me
better than planned maintenance
and A&E was a good walk

Urgent
two days and you're off
so where's the poem
to slip in your kitbag
camouflaged by bandages
as you treat the effects
of snipers and IEDs

to remind you of home
the normal worries
of slugs and spiders

the corridors were blank

the relaxed intensity
of the Resus Room a release
till the job was done
and Sister suggested toast

you're in the kitchen
this morning
spreading thick brown slices
a round each
and in the way of words
a word sticks
forcing an image
where you're taking a round
from a stranger's gut

that's your job
like this was mine
but you'll only get out
to some makeshift NAAFI
too tired to write
wanting those other smells
to be overwhelmed
by some lines to tell you
there's still no slugs and spiders.

Couples

One
Gets a table
One
Joins the queue
Leaving me
Standing
With a tray
And a terrible
Sense of injustice

Convincing Irene

There's five technicians
crammed in the office
one wants fags
two want whisky
one wants matches
from the bar at Raffles
but I want something different.

That's why I'm at the back
leaning on a filing cabinet
checking the post
as she shows photos
of her son's flat
avoiding her look
and another discussion
where I tell her the facts
about contrails
killing farmers in Bangladesh
and I might slip in
something about Peak Oil
if she's still listening
and I haven't lost it.

And she won't be listening
and I will lose it
as she tells me once again
that something will turn up
and I'll storm out
knowing it's cost me
a trip to the florist
and worst of all
I can't give a damn
about the price of apologies
or the cost of their bloody carbon footprint.

Teahouse on the Hill, Lincoln
(for Anne Drinkell)

What with the excitement
of an extra scone
it completely slipped my mind
to tell you the waitress
had told me the décor
was changed in March

actually she said stripped
with a degree of enthusiasm
that would have the girls giggling
so it was lucky they weren't there
when you found what you found
on the door of the cathedral
and can you imagine
trying to explain that snakes
don't usually end up
where they ended up there

though it seems
from what you were saying
there's a few where you work
that could shed a skin
and preferably yours
so don't think I'm prying
but there must be times
when you feel like that chap
at the table by the window
pretending to read the menu
while his teapot's untouched

and that's what this is about
one of us stirring the other's pot
adding milk and sugar

when the other doesn't care
we've been there before
and now we've been here
and where we go next
goes with a hug from the other
not from those anacondas
squeezing the life out of you

and talking of them
just think of those masons
that twelfth century porn
cutting snakes into stone
well we won't need chisels
but I think I can safely say
the result will be much the same
do you want that butter.

Sending Groceries

A few luxuries
once a week
seemed more than fair
which is why on Mondays
I'd clear the desk
create a space

and contemplate a box
of ten silver sachets of Cappuccino
(with chocolate topping)
assorted slim selections of biscuits
a packet of fruit gums
and an A5 envelope

which is why by Monday evening
there'd be a floor full of stuff
surplus to requirements
and an odd shaped lump
plastered with stamps

addressed to abbreviations
of rank and number
at a BFPO where NAAFIs
supplied the basics of life
while you did the same
in twelve hour shifts.

Flirting

Flirt:
Origin obscure
possibly connected to *fleureter*
to talk sweet nothing

the icing on my cake
of day to day work
where an ECG is drifting
or I point out a fault
to the Sister in Charge

making it fun
knowing the limits
leaving the ward with her smile
tucked in my tool case

knowing the limits
knowing it doesn't work
when the Staff Nurse is twenty five
and I'm...well...
I'm not.

It's time to go
the job is changing
and so am I
it's time to work on
shy and retiring.

Ironing Curtains

Pausing
to turn a difficult crease
the iron gives a soft sigh
letting me know its confusion
over patterns shaping
out of material itself confused.

Seeing problems with further progress
I sit on the stair and try to explain
about cause and effect
and the use of symbols and imagery
until stopped by a groaning sound
from the board beneath.

Undeterred
I stand
and move in front of the mirror
pointing out
with reference to a photograph
how change in appearance
can be a symbol
perhaps of change itself
perhaps of growth.

Perhaps it was time to stop
as I could tell that concepts
involving beards and growth
were too much for an iron
used to resting on Saturday nights

and the curtain
whilst attracted to the idea of symbols
was slowly losing interest
and looked tired as night drew in.

Switching on the light
I smiled and merely mentioned
pulling ourselves together.

Christmas Present

Back home
at this time of night
it would be Christmas Day
deep and crisp and
even if it were raining
the sound of pattering
would be tiptoeing kids
not the a/c's occasional tap

back home
at this time of night
the lights on the tree
would be off
and all those soft colours
all those lines dripping
from its slim trunk
would not be turning red

and the boxes
you've ripped the wrapping off
would have chocolate biscuits
or a sweater from M&S
so pity the poor aunt
who sent pairs of socks
to this victim of an IED

there's no time
to think about presents
you're not Santa selecting
the good boys and girls
and anyway all you have
is a single gift to give
it's all you want to give
and all that's wanted
this gift of life.

M's Request for an Erotic Poem

I've put a photograph on my desk,
just in front of me,
just for this,
it's not needed,
you're on a window seat reading,
a hotel in the Lakes,
white sweater,
blue jeans,
feet crossed on cushions,
bare feet crossed on cushions.
I've never tired of it.

mobile phones

by the time
we got to the hotel
he'd phoned home twice
excusing himself
which amused me
and I wanted to tell you

by the time
we got to Wednesday
he was on five a day
and I missed you

by Friday
I heard your voice
from every passing phone

every passing stranger
calling home
about leaking taps
or dental appointments
while I thought about you
me and you

in the monotony
of mobile phones
I began to understand passion.

Homecoming

The Service

A simple space
disguised in early Gothic
flying buttresses
carrying the weight
of being St Nicks
the sailor's church
who've probably nipped out
for a fag and cappuccino
as top brass rub shoulders
with Colonels and Corporals
camouflaged in pews
in a uniformed mass
till the sound of a civvie
taking a photo
turns the head
of a Sergeant who's sensed
a fiancé's touch
and a smile flashes
through family and friends
into eyes where it truly belongs.

Freedom of the City

Following the band
and the march through streets
where applause from crowds
rattles in rounds
that a month before
was another surge
of ripped bodies
wrapped in khaki or cotton
another round of morphine

the grip of a hand
as it slowly lets go
no time to think
of a day like today
side by side
moving as one
through the freedom of the city.

Presentation

Close order
Right dress
between St George's
and Lime Street Station
three lines
for the Mayor to walk
to stop for a chat
or present a medal
to embarrassed soldiers
as their shy families
find themselves whooping
behind lenses and a barricade
three lines recalling
the words of the Padre
in that Liverpool Church

and now these three remain
faith, hope and love

I find no sin in pride
as they fall out
and a special face smiles
ready to come home

but the greatest of these is love.

Credo

I believe in God
Creator of heaven and earth,
In Zeus, King of the Gods, sky and air,
Son of Cronus, born of Rhea,
I believe in Jupiter
King of the Gods, sky and storm,
In Ra, the sun God,
In Toci, Goddess of Earth,
Rhiannon, Goddess of Moon,
I believe in Odin, King of the Gods,
Son of Bestia and Borr,
I believe in the Trinity,
Father, Son and Holy Spirit,
In Brahma, the Supreme Deity,
In Allah, the one God,
I believe I am that I am,
In Nonak and Gurus,
I believe in Joseph Smith and angels,
In mediums and spirits,
I and I believe in God incarnate,
In Merlin and magic spells,
In faeries and magic glades,
I believe in Dan Brown,
The communion of myths
The force of mystery
The power of words
The question of being
and the amen of knowledge
The amen of knowledge.

Indigo Dreams Publishing
132, Hinckley Road
Stoney Stanton
Leicestershire
LE9 4LN
www.indigodreams.co.uk